Short Stack Editions | Volume 9

Plums

by Martha Holmberg

Short Stack Editions

Publisher: Nick Fau
Creative Director: Rotem Raffe
Editor: Kaitlyn Goalen
Copy Editor: Abby Tannenbaum
Business Manager: Mackenzie Smith

ISBN 978-0-9896017-8-8

Printed in New York City
July 2014

Table of Contents

Preserves

Sweet and savory are the black and white of the cooking world: To be solely one or the other is easy, but limiting. In the kitchen, as in life, the magic usually occurs somewhere in the gray area.

For many, plums are one-dimensional sugar grenades, considered a snack in their raw state. At best, they hold court as a fixture of dessert, but even then they're overshadowed by their fuzzy cousin, the peach.

In this edition, Martha Holmberg places plums squarely in the middle of the spectrum, etching out a newfound depth for these sultry stone fruits. Some recipes reveal how the fruit can benefit from a savory treatment, while others pay homage to the plum's unequivocal sweetness.

Part of the joy of an ingredient-driven cookbook series is the thrill of discovery. Our authors' love for their chosen muses acts as a key, unlocking an ingredient from its perceived limitations and demonstrating its reach and versatility. Thanks to Martha, a new door to plums has been opened, shining bright new light into our kitchens.

—The Editors

Introduction

I fell in love with plums only after I became an adult, and although I wish I could share stories of a childhood filled with trips to Grandpa's orchards and visions of Mom's pies cooling on the counter, my early food experiences were more prosaic than poetic.

My dad was a naval officer and my mom did her shopping at the commissary, where she could buy the most food for the fewest dollars. In our house, fresh fruit amounted to seedless grapes, Red Delicious apples (which they are not, by the way) and the occasional banana. A ripe, juicy plum was a pleasure not yet mine.

After college, I moved to Paris. I acquired an older and slightly sketchy French boyfriend, started drinking Rhône wine, dipping my buttered baguette into my morning café au lait and eating real (fresh, in season, delectable) fruit.

On one visit to my neighborhood market, I bought a punnet of unassuming greenish-gold plums called Reine Claudes (who else but the French would have a queen named Claude?). Though I might risk being a cliché, I have to say that I took one bite and my life was changed. And now here I am writing a book about plums. Thank God for bad French boyfriends.

The plum is an under-the-radar fruit. The beauty of a plum becomes apparent when it is quietly contemplated, but isn't as obvious as, say, a fat crimson strawberry, a bosomy peach or an exotic blood orange. Plums are mostly all the same shape—round, with an occasional teardrop or oval sneaking in—with smooth surfaces that conceal the luscious flesh inside.

But a plum's modesty belies its sensual nature. We plum aficionados know the fine snap of biting through taut, thin skin into supremely juicy flesh, the immediate sweet-tart quench, not to mention the overall efficiency of the fruit: no peeling necessary, no stem to twist off and only a tiny pit to discard. Hey, I'm the daughter of a Swedish naval aviator. I think efficiency is sexy!

Plums also play well with savory ingredients—such as chiles, onions, herbs and assertive spices—and just about all meat and poultry, integrating into a savory main course without feeling like a novelty. And when a plum meets heat, you get a whole new level of deliciousness. Juices flow, flesh softens, colors get crazy vivid. I think plums are one of the few fruits that are even better cooked than raw.

My affection for plums began in Paris, but then it grew into a fullblown obsession after I moved to Portland, Oregon, where I first encountered wild plums. A remarkable potato grower from eastern Oregon (Gene Thiel, who died recently, bless him) would bring a few paper bags of wild plums to the market along with his potatoes and carrots. His table was earth-colored and gnarly except for these gem-toned beauties. They ranged from marble to ping-pongball size, from celadon to orchid to magenta and had a flavor that led with sour but followed with something ancient and poetic and compelling.

I always bought up all that Gene had, usually only a pound or two, and then treated myself to an afternoon of watching the glossy fruit cook into a jam full of sunset colors, French sensuality and the essence of my true favorite, the plum.

—*Martha Holmberg*

Recipes

How to Choose
Your Plums

Plums have many fanciful names and come in colors ranging from lettuce green to obsidian blue-black, but I've found that the actual variety doesn't really matter that much. What matters: the juiciness and flavor of the individual plum.

For eating out of hand, you'll want something that feels plump and heavy and yields to the touch, meaning the flesh is likely to be sweet and moist. For salads and salsas, look for a firmer, tarter plum, which will keep its shape and texture better.

Although variety isn't crucial—I've developed the recipes in this book to work well with most any plum—I do want to point out a few types that have distinctive characters. If you see these in your market, give them a try and get to know their personalities.

Shiro plums

I love these partly thanks to their translucent pale-yellow skin and partly due to flavor that's delicately poised between sweet and tart and the flesh that's juicy but never mushy. I like to add a few Shiros to my plum jams.

Big, fat, reddish-purple plums

This description applies to plums of many colors and names, which don't differ much from one another in flavor and texture. They all can be marvelous, so try to taste before you buy.

Italian prune plums

These are better for cooking than eating raw. They tend to be drier and can be ever so slightly mealy when they're raw (mealy fruit is a cardinal sin). Italian plums are bluish purple, small and oval—almost like a Roma tomato. Excellent for galettes and cakes, these plums are flavorful but not too juicy, so they won't make the pastry soggy.

The Reine Claude plums

The variety that started it all for me. These are also called greengage plums; they're not that easy to find in the United States, but they're totally worth seeking out (or growing, as I do in my small urban yard. Who needs Grandpa's orchards, I ask you?) Greengage plums are small, greenish-gold and fairly firm but with a densely luscious flesh that's perfumed and sweetly floral. Gorgeous in a tart or compote, this plum would be lovely in one of the salad recipes as well.

Pluots

A new plum-apricot hybrid, with a name better suited to particle physics than to food, pluots are showing up in a lot of markets. Despite the dumb name, I think they're just fine, and they can be substituted for traditional plums in my recipes. The flesh and flavor is much closer to a plum than an apricot. Thank goodness.

Grilled Pancetta-Wrapped Plum Wedges

At a cocktail party, when the tray with the ubiquitous bacon-wrapped date appetizer comes around, I hesitate—those intensely sweet-salty nuggets can be cloying, and they don't play nicely with my glass of wine. These plum hors d'oeuvres, however, are light and fresh, even with their crispy meat jacket. I like to use packaged pancetta because the superthin slices are easy to wrap around the plums, and they crisp up nicely.

½ cup balsamic vinegar

2 ripe-but-firm large plums (or 4 small), pitted and cut into wedges

Kosher salt and freshly ground black pepper

3 ounces very thinly sliced pancetta

In a small saucepan over medium heat, boil the vinegar until it's reduced by half to a syrupy glaze. Let cool.

Season the plum wedges generously with salt and pepper. Wrap each wedge with some of the pancetta so that the plum is covered.

Arrange a medium-hot fire on your grill or heat the broiler and place the rack about 4 inches away from the heat. Set the plums on the grill grate (with the pancetta seam-side down) or on a baking sheet and grill or broil until the pancetta is browned and starting to sizzle and crisp and the plums are softened, about 2 minutes a side.

Let the plums cool slightly, drizzle with a tiny bit of the balsamic glaze and serve as finger food.

Arugula Salad with Plums & Pancetta

I love using plums in salads because, even when they're quite ripe, plums are bright and acidic (in a good way). This encourages the wonderful tension of sweet-salty-sour that compels you to take another bite. If you can't find aged Gouda, which is fairly dry with a toffee-like quality, use Parmigiano-Reggiano.

2 ounces pancetta, finely chopped

2 tablespoons white wine vinegar

½ teaspoon Dijon mustard

Kosher salt and freshly ground black pepper

¼ cup fruity extra-virgin olive oil

6 cups loosely packed arugula—large stems removed, leaves washed and thoroughly dried

2 ripe large plums, pitted and cut into small chunks or thin wedges

3 ounces aged Gouda, cut into thin strips (about 1 cup)—it's okay if they break apart

1 ounce pecans, toasted and coarsely chopped (about ¼ cup)

serves
·4·

Place the pancetta in a small skillet and cook over medium-low heat, stirring occasionally, until crisp and browned, about 5 minutes. Transfer to a paper-towel-lined plate. (Save the rendered fat in the skillet for another use; it's too delicious to waste.)

In a small bowl, whisk together the vinegar, mustard, ¼ teaspoon of salt and ⅛ teaspoon of pepper. Slowly whisk in the oil until the vinaigrette is emulsified and smooth.

Place the arugula and plums in a large bowl and toss gently to coat with half of the vinaigrette; divide among four plates. Top each with some of the cheese, then drizzle with a little of the remaining dressing. Sprinkle the pancetta and pecans over the top and serve right away.

Baked Plums with Savory Cheese Streusel

I love the tender crunch and buttery flavor of a streusel topping so much that I decided to steer it into savory territory here. The virtues that baked plums bring to dessert—namely a sweet-tart juiciness—are equally good in this first course or light lunch that hovers between savory and sweet. When you pit the plums, use a melon baller to create a nice shallow cavity in the plum halves to hold some of the streusel.

¼ cup unbleached all-purpose flour

⅓ cup grated aged sharp cheddar cheese

1½ tablespoons unsalted butter, cut into pieces

¼ cup toasted slivered almonds

½ teaspoon fresh thyme leaves

Pinch of cayenne pepper

Kosher salt and freshly ground black pepper

4 ripe-but-firm medium plums, halved and pitted

1 tablespoon fruity extra-virgin olive oil

½ teaspoon sugar

4 small handfuls (about 4 cups) of salad greens, for serving, dressed (right before serving) with just a few drops of balsamic vinegar and olive oil

serves
-4-

Heat the oven to 425°.

In a food processor, pulse the flour, cheese, butter, almonds, thyme, cayenne, ¼ teaspoon of salt and a few grinds of pepper until the mixture looks like coarse meal. Dump it out onto a work surface, then pinch and squeeze it with your fingers until it forms little clumps.

Toss the plum halves with the olive oil in a medium bowl. Season with salt, pepper and the sugar, then arrange them, cut-side up, in a small baking dish that holds them in a snug single layer.

Crumble the streusel over the plums. Bake until the plums soften and begin getting juicy and the streusel is deep golden with a bit of brown around the edges and rather crunchy, 15 to 20 minutes.

Let the plums cool until warm but no longer hot. Divide them among four salad plates on top of a bed of the lightly dressed greens and serve.

Beet Salad with Plums, Basil & Feta

The addition of plums is my way of freshening up this classic beet salad. I find that the flavor of ripe plums plays nicely with sweet, minerally beets, and the similarity in color creates a kind of visual puzzle. Try to find feta made from sheep's milk or a blend of sheep and goat; the flavor is sweet and mellow and better suited to this salad than the aggressively tangy varieties.

1 pound medium beets, trimmed and scrubbed

Kosher salt

2 tablespoons fruity extra-virgin olive oil

2 teaspoons finely grated lime zest

1 tablespoon fresh lime juice

1 tablespoon sherry vinegar

½ teaspoon honey

Freshly ground black pepper

Cayenne pepper or hot sauce

2 ripe medium plums (about 8 ounces), pitted and cut into ½-inch chunks

2 tablespoons lightly packed very thinly sliced basil leaves

½ cup crumbled feta cheese

serves
4

Add 1 inch of water to a large saucepan and place a steamer insert or basket inside the pan. Add the beets, cover and steam over low heat until a paring knife enters them easily, about 30 to 45 minutes, depending on their size. Set the beets aside until they're cool enough to handle but still warm. Peel the beets (the skin will rub right off) and cut them into ½-inch chunks, then transfer to a large bowl. Season lightly with salt.

In a small bowl, whisk the oil with the lime zest, lime juice, vinegar and honey. Season generously with salt, pepper and a pinch of cayenne (or a dash of hot sauce). Taste the dressing, and if it's not zesty enough, add a little more vinegar.

Add the plums to the bowl of beets and toss gently with the dressing. Refrigerate for at least 15 and up to 30 minutes.

Pile the salad onto a large platter or in a wide bowl, scatter the basil and feta over the top and serve cool but not ice cold.

Plums in Black Pepper-Balsamic Vinaigrette

A few years ago, I realized that I hate "fruit salad," which is frequently just a thoughtless jumble of fresh fruit that somehow landed in a bowl. Instead, I've begun making my fruit salads like this one: a tailored selection of fruit—in this case, just one—with a vinaigrette that makes the plums taste even more quenchy-juicy. Add a little mint and the salad becomes sophisticated and delicious. It's also a bit of a chameleon, equally satisfying as a light dessert as it is an accompaniment to grilled steak or barbecued chicken. Use a mix of plum varieties for the prettiest color, and try adding some fragrant basil along with the mint for a more complex perfume.

serves -4-

3 tablespoons fresh orange juice

1 tablespoon balsamic vinegar

1 teaspoon sugar

Kosher salt and freshly ground black pepper

⅛ teaspoon ground cardamom

1 tablespoon thinly sliced mint leaves

2 tablespoons fruity extra-virgin olive oil

1 pound ripe plums (about 4 medium), pitted and cut into thin wedges

In a large bowl, whisk together the orange juice, balsamic vinegar, sugar, ¼ teaspoon of salt, ⅛ teaspoon of pepper and the cardamom until the sugar and salt have dissolved. Add half of the mint, then whisk in the oil, a few drops at a time, until the vinaigrette has emulsified and is creamy. Taste the dressing and adjust the seasoning so there's a nice interplay of sweet, sour and salty.

Add the plums to the vinaigrette and gently toss. Let them sit for at least 15 minutes (but no longer than 1 hour). Just before serving, taste the plums and adjust with more vinegar, sugar, salt or pepper, then gently toss with the remaining mint.

Little Birds with Rye-Plum Stuffing

Plums play two roles in this simple stuffing: They provide a nice pop of brightness in an otherwise earthy mixture, and they add moisture to the stuffing by collapsing and releasing juice as they cook. Rye bread gives this an Eastern European feeling, like something I'd eat while holing up at a cozy Polish farmhouse. I like this stuffing with Cornish game hens, but it's also wonderful with larger birds such as chicken, duck or even a small turkey (if you're taking the turkey route, double the recipe).

2 ounces thick-cut bacon (about 2 slices), cut into 1-inch pieces

5 tablespoons unsalted butter, softened, divided

1 cup chopped yellow onion

1 cup chopped celery

2 tablespoons chopped rosemary, divided

2 tablespoons chopped thyme leaves, divided

Kosher salt and freshly ground black pepper

3 ripe medium plums (about 12 ounces), pitted and cut into ½-inch chunks (about 1½ cups)

6 ounces hearty rye bread, cut into ½-inch cubes (about 4 cups)

¼ cup low-sodium or homemade chicken broth, more as needed

4 Cornish game hens or small poussins (about 14 ounces each)

White wine, chicken broth or water, for deglazing the pan (optional)

serves
-4-

Position a rack in the center of the oven and heat the oven to 400°.

Cook the bacon in a large skillet over medium heat until it has rendered much of its fat and is starting to become crisp, 3 to 5 minutes. Pour off all but about 1 tablespoon of the fat; save the extra fat for cooking your next batch of eggs.

Return the skillet to medium heat and melt 3 tablespoons of the butter in it. Add the onion, celery, half the rosemary and half the thyme; stir to coat. Season generously with salt and pepper. Cook, stirring occasionally, until the vegetables are very soft and fragrant, but not browned, 8 to 10 minutes. Add the plums and cook, stirring often, for just a minute or two until they soften slightly. Stir in the bread and combine well, then add the chicken broth and mix gently. Season to taste with more salt and pepper. The stuffing should be moist but not soggy; if it seems a little dry, add more broth. Note that if you're baking the stuffing outside of a bird, it should be slightly moister.

Remove anything unexpected from the cavities of the birds (such as bags of giblets) and loosely fill each with the stuffing. Depending on the size of your birds, you may have some stuffing left over, which you can pack into a few buttered ramekins and bake alongside the birds.

Rub the skin of the birds with the remaining 2 tablespoons of butter and season with the remaining rosemary and thyme and a generous shower of salt and pepper. Arrange the birds on a rack in a large roasting pan and cook until the flesh is very tender and the juices run completely clear, 40 to 60 minutes. Let the birds rest for at least 10 minutes before serving.

If there is leftover juice in the roasting pan, pour off any fat and deglaze the pan with a bit of white wine and/or chicken broth (or even water), using a wooden spoon to scrape up any flavorful browned bits. Bring to a boil, whisking often, and cook until the liquid is concentrated in flavor. Serve the jus with the birds.

Roasted Chicken with Plums, Onions & Herbs

This dish is what a cooking friend of mine calls a "walk-away dish." You basically shove it in the oven, walk away and, when you come back, dinner is ready. I usually roast the chicken thighs in a half-sheet pan (a heavy baking sheet with a rim), which catches the juices. The secret is to make sure the ingredients have room to spread out, so it's better to use multiple pans than risk crowding the ingredients, or they'll steam instead of roast.

1 pound ripe medium plums (about 4), pitted and cut into eighths

1 large red onion, sliced ¼-inch thick

¼ cup extra-virgin olive oil

¼ teaspoon crushed red pepper flakes or ⅛ teaspoon cayenne pepper

1 tablespoon coarsely chopped thyme

1 tablespoon coarsely chopped rosemary

Kosher salt and freshly ground black pepper

4 bone-in, skin-on chicken thighs (about 1½ pounds total)

serves ·4·

Position a rack in the center of the oven and heat the oven to 425°.

In a large bowl, combine the plums, onion, oil, pepper flakes, thyme, rosemary and 1 teaspoon of salt.

Season the chicken thighs generously on both sides with salt and pepper. Arrange the chicken on a heavy-duty rimmed baking sheet, leaving space between the pieces. Distribute the plum and onion mixture around the chicken.

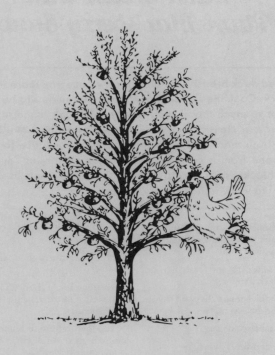

Roast until the chicken is tender and its juices run clear when pierced with a knife, 40 to 45 minutes. Check on the plums a couple of times during cooking; you want the plums and onions to release their juices, collapse and brown slightly but not to burn onto the pan. If they're getting too dark too quickly, add a few spoonfuls of water to the pan.

When the chicken is done, arrange it on a platter. If there's a lot of rendered chicken fat on the plums, spoon it off and save for another use. Arrange the plums around the chicken. If there are nice browned bits and juice on the baking sheet, deglaze it with a splash of water, scraping up any bits with a wooden spoon, and pour over the plums. Serve warm.

Duck Breast with Plum-Blackberry Sauce

Sautéed duck breast is an easy luxury once you learn the following trick: Cook the skin so that enough fat remains to be succulent but not so much that it feels flabby. Although this dish is a long way from a classic duck à l'Orange, it has the same basic elements: rich meat and a slightly sharp, fruity sauce that gets its backbone from a caramel-and-vinegar gastrique. I'm including some blackberries here because I think both fruits have enough acidity to work well in savory dishes.

2 boneless, skin-on moulard duck breast halves (about 1 pound total)

Kosher salt and freshly ground black pepper

2 tablespoons chopped thyme and/or rosemary

1 tablespoon sugar

¼ cup sherry vinegar

1 firm-ripe large plum, pitted and diced (about 1 cup)

½ cup fresh or thawed frozen blackberries

1 tablespoon finely chopped shallot

1 teaspoon finely chopped, cored and seeded hot fresh chile, such as jalapeño

½ cup low-sodium or homemade chicken broth (or duck broth!)

1 teaspoon unsalted butter

serves 2 to 3

Use a sharp knife to lightly score through the skin and fat of the duck breasts in a crosshatch pattern; this helps render the fat and crisp the skin. Season the duck all over with 1 teaspoon of salt, generous grinds of pepper and the thyme and/or rosemary. Place the breasts on a plate, cover and refrigerate for at least an hour and up to 1 day.

When you're ready to cook, blot the duck completely dry with a paper towel (don't worry if some of the seasoning comes off). Heat a large heavy-duty skillet over medium-high heat until very hot. Add the duck breasts, skin-side down, then adjust the heat so that the duck sizzles quietly. Don't let it smoke. Cook the breasts, undisturbed, until a lot of the fat has rendered and the skin is browned and crisp, about 5 minutes, depending on the thickness of the fat layer. (If there's a lot of accumulated fat in the pan, carefully pour it off into a container and save it to cook wonderful things later on.)

Flip the breasts and continue cooking until they're just slightly past rare (or when an instant-read thermometer inserted into the thickest part of the breast registers 120°; they'll continue to cook while you make the sauce), 3 to 5 minutes longer. Transfer to a plate, cover loosely with foil and let rest.

Pour off the remaining duck fat, return the skillet to medium heat and sprinkle the sugar over the bottom of the skillet in an even layer. Cook until it begins to melt and caramelize, shaking the pan as needed to avoid dark spots from forming; you want the sugar to be a deep-amber color. As soon as most of the sugar has caramelized, add the vinegar (stand back, its aroma will clear your sinuses) and let it reduce for a few seconds. Add the plums, blackberries, shallot and chile. Stir the fruit around to coat it with sugar; continue to cook, stirring, until the fruit starts to break up and all the flavors mix together. Add the chicken broth, turn the heat to high and cook the sauce until the plums and berries collapse and get juicy and the shallots and chile soften, about 3 to 4 minutes longer. Whisk in the butter, then taste and season with more salt and pepper so that the sauce is quite savory.

To serve, pour any duck juice that has accumulated on the plate into the sauce. Slice the duck crosswise into ¼-inch-thick slices and serve with a ribbon of the sauce, with more on the side.

Sautéed Pork Tenderloin with Prunes & Capers

This type of sautéed-and-deglazed dish always makes me happy when I'm cooking during the workweek, as it evokes fanciness with minimal effort. And we all need a bit of midweek luxury, I believe. I'm making the dish with prunes (we all know that prunes are dried plums, right?) instead of fresh plums because I love the dark, complex sweetness of prunes. It's almost liquor-like, which works beautifully with sweet pork. The capers give those sweet ingredients a nice briny kick for contrast. This recipe also works well with boneless, skinless chicken thighs.

4 ounces pitted prunes

½ cup dry, unoaked white wine (such as Grüner Veltliner)

One 14-ounce pork tenderloin, trimmed of any silver skin and cut crosswise into 1-inch-thick medallions

Kosher salt and freshly ground black pepper

All-purpose flour, for dredging

1 tablespoon extra-virgin olive oil

1 tablespoon unsalted butter

1 tablespoon finely chopped shallot

¾ cup low-sodium or homemade chicken broth

¼ cup heavy cream or crème fraîche

2 tablespoons capers, rinsed and drained

Chopped parsley or chervil, for garnish

serves 2 to 3

In a small saucepan, bring the prunes and wine to a boil. Lower the heat and simmer very gently for about 10 minutes, then remove from the heat and let the prunes steep for another 20 minutes or so, until they are very tender. (You can do this while you're prepping the rest of the dish.) Drain the prunes through a fine-mesh strainer placed over a bowl, reserving the prunes and wine separately.

Using the palm of your hand, gently press the tenderloin medallions into an even thickness, then season them well with salt and pepper. Lightly dredge each medallion in flour, tapping off the excess.

Heat the oil and butter in a large heavy-duty skillet over medium-high heat. When the fats are very hot—but not smoking—add the pork and cook, turning once, until nicely browned on both sides with just a whisper of pink left in the middle, 2 to 3 minutes a side (the pork will continue to cook a bit after it's off the heat). Transfer the pork to a platter or dinner plates and cover with foil to keep warm.

Return the skillet to the heat, add the shallot and cook, stirring, until softened but not at all brown, about 1 minute. Add the reserved wine and deglaze the pan; use a wooden spoon to scrape up any browned bits so they dissolve. Simmer until the wine has reduced to about 1 tablespoon of glaze (this will happen quickly). Add the chicken broth and any pork juice that has accumulated on the platter and continue boiling until the sauce has reduced to about ¼ cup. Whisk in the cream, simmer another few seconds, then add the capers and season to taste with salt and pepper. Be sure to remove the pan from the heat once your sauce is ready, otherwise it will keep cooking and disappear before your eyes.

Place the pork on a platter, nestle the prunes around it, then drizzle the sauce over the top. Garnish with chopped parsley or chervil and serve.

Spiced Lamb Kebabs with Iranian-Style Rice

This dish shares DNA with a classic Iranian recipe called *albaloo polow*, which is made with sour cherries. I first encountered it when my Parisian cooking-school friend roomed with two Persian brothers. It seemed so exotic to me—fruit and saffron and a slightly magical crust on the rice? Definitely not Escoffier.

Since then, I've experimented with sour cherries (when I can get them), sweet cherries, plums and, most recently, "sour plums": small, green plums that I found at a Lebanese market. These plums stay tart and crunchy even when they're ripe, and they show up in many Middle Eastern and Eastern European cuisines in various ways, though it seems that everyone likes to dip the raw plums in salt and eat them as a snack.

Pay attention to this rice-cooking method, which yields extremely long and fluffy grains and the prized *tadig*—a crispy layer of rice that forms on the bottom of the pot. You don't always get a proper *tadig*, but when you do, you feel like a genius cook. The spice rub would also be delicious on beef or dark-meat chicken.

For the lamb:

2 garlic cloves, minced or finely grated

1 tablespoon pomegranate molasses

1 teaspoon sumac or ½ teaspoon fresh lemon juice

¼ teaspoon ground cinnamon

¼ teaspoon ground allspice

½ teaspoon ground cumin

½ teaspoon Aleppo pepper or other fruity ground hot chile

Kosher salt and freshly ground black pepper

1 pound lamb sirloin, cut into 1-inch chunks

serves 2 to 3

-26-

For the plums:

12 ounces sour green plums, pitted and cut into chunks (or 2 large ripe plums, pitted and cut into ½-inch chunks)

2 tablespoons seeded and minced poblano or other moderately hot fresh green chile

2 tablespoons minced shallot or yellow onion

1 teaspoon to 1 tablespoon sugar

Kosher salt

¼ cup cilantro leaves (optional)

For the rice:

1½ cups basmati rice

Kosher salt

5 tablespoons unsalted butter

½ teaspoon saffron threads soaked in 2 tablespoons of hot water

¼ cup fresh cilantro leaves

Marinate the lamb: Stir the garlic, molasses, sumac, cinnamon, allspice, cumin, Aleppo pepper, ½ teaspoon of salt and ¼ teaspoon of pepper in a large bowl to combine; add the lamb and toss to coat, massaging the spice mix into the meat with your fingers. Set the meat aside at room temperature for up to 1 hour or cover and refrigerate for up to 24 hours.

Marinate the plums: Toss the plums, chile, shallot, sugar (1 tablespoon if using sour plums, 1 teaspoon if using ripe plums), ½ teaspoon of salt and the cilantro, if using. Set the plums aside at room temperature to marinate while the rice soaks. (If you're using sour plums, place the ingredients listed above in a skillet and cook over medium heat until the plums soften slightly, about 5 minutes. Don't let the chile or shallot brown.)

Make the rice: Soak the rice in cold water for at least 15 and up to 30 minutes, then drain well. Bring a large pot of generously salted water to a boil, stir in the rice and boil for exactly 8 minutes. Drain through a fine-mesh strainer right away.

Melt the butter in the pot you used to cook the rice. Pour most of the butter over the plum mixture, leaving a nice coating of butter on the bottom of the pot. Add half of the drained rice to the pot, drizzle half of the saffron and its soaking water over it, then layer on half of the plum mixture. Continue layering the remaining rice, saffron mixture and plum mixture.

Wrap a kitchen towel around the lid of the pot and cover the pot with the lid to form an airtight seal. Cook the rice over high heat just to get the steam going, about 1 minute once it gets hot; reduce the heat to its very lowest level and cook for another 10 minutes. Remove the lid, raise the heat slightly and continue cooking for a few more minutes to develop a light crust on the bottom of the pan, but try not to burn the bottom—it's a bit of a dance.

Meanwhile, place an oven rack about 4 inches below the broiler element and heat the broiler to high. Thread the lamb onto long skewers (if the skewers are wooden, soak them in water for 30 minutes before using them) and broil until the meat is rosy in the middle, turning once, 7 to 8 minutes total.

Pile the rice and plums and all of the crust from the bottom of the pot onto a platter. Top with the lamb kebabs and any juices that have accumulated in the pan. Shower with the cilantro and serve.

Maple-and-Rum-Poached Prunes with Ice Cream

A message to my fellow rum-raisin lovers: Don't waste your time with measly raisins because you can now have succulent, complexly sweet prunes...and maple syrup, too. The classic duo becomes a trio and turns plain ice cream into a remarkable dessert. I prefer to use grade B maple syrup for its delicious toasty caramel flavor, but grade A will work just fine. Do take care that the prunes don't soak up all the liquid, which can happen with very dry fruit. If that occurs, add a few spoonfuls of water to loosen up the topping.

8 ounces pitted prunes, halved	Kosher salt	*serves* · 4 ·
⅓ cup maple syrup (preferably grade B)	Good-quality coffee and/or vanilla ice cream	
⅓ cup dark rum (Myers is a good choice)	½ cup chopped toasted almonds	

In small a saucepan, combine the prunes with the maple syrup, rum, ⅓ cup of water and a pinch of salt and bring to a simmer. Turn off the heat and let the prunes soak until they are very soft, 20 minutes to 1 hour, depending on how dry they are.

Using a slotted spoon, transfer the prunes to a plate; leave the liquid in the saucepan. Bring it to a simmer and cook until it is syrupy, 4 to 5 minutes. Cool slightly, then chill the syrup in the fridge until it's completely cold.

Put a scoop or two of ice cream in each bowl and spoon the prunes and syrup over the top. Sprinkle with the almonds and serve immediately.

Note: Make a double batch of the prunes and keep them in the refrigerator for up to three weeks so you can spoon them over a slice of almond cake or dip a madeleine into the syrup. Or put some into a jar with a ribbon and bring them to your neighbor.

Creamy Ricotta
with Plum Compote

This dish proves that dessert doesn't need to be decadent to be delicious. Here, it's all about the moment that the milky-sweet purity of the ricotta meets the deep fruitiness of the compote—a gorgeous contrast in colors, textures and flavors. You can prepare both components a day or so ahead, making this a convenient dessert for a dinner party or brunch.

16 ounces whole-milk ricotta

½ cup heavy cream

2 tablespoons confectioners' sugar

½ teaspoon pure vanilla extract

4 ripe medium plums (about 1 pound), pitted and cut into small chunks

¼ cup sugar, plus more as needed

⅛ teaspoon ground cardamom

⅛ teaspoon ground cinnamon

Fresh lemon juice

Butter cookies, for serving (optional)

serves
·4·

Line a fine-mesh strainer with a double layer of paper towels or cheesecloth. Set the strainer over a medium bowl so that the bottom of the strainer doesn't touch the bottom of the bowl. Spoon the ricotta into the strainer, cover the whole contraption with plastic wrap and let drain in the refrigerator overnight.

Pour off and discard the whey in the bowl (or add it to a smoothie!) and reserve the ricotta. In a large bowl, whip the cream and confectioners' sugar until the cream holds very soft peaks, then add the vanilla. Gently fold the ricotta into the cream, then chill until you're ready to serve.

Meanwhile, combine the plums, sugar, cardamom, cinnamon, a few drops of lemon juice and a tablespoon or so of water in a large skillet over medium-high heat. Bring to a gentle simmer, stirring at first to dissolve the sugar.

Cook, uncovered, until the plums begin to fall apart and the juice has thickened, 8 to 10 minutes. If the plums are really disintegrating but the juice is still thin, scrape the plums into a bowl, leaving the juice in the pan; boil the juice until nicely thickened. Reunite the plums and juice, then taste and adjust with more sugar or lemon juice. Let the compote cool, then transfer to the refrigerator and chill.

Scoop some of the ricotta mixture into four bowls and top with the compote. Serve alongside a plate of butter cookies for something crunchy, if you like.

Plum-Frangipane Tartlets with Brown Sugar & Almonds

Frangipane, a sweet almond filling, is a magic substance when it comes to fruit desserts—and stone fruit in particular. Plums and their brethren have high juice contents, which can soak into your crust and make it soggy. Here, the frangipane acts like a delicious sponge, shielding the crust by absorbing excess juice. I use frozen puff pastry, but if you prefer to make your own, please do.

Unsalted butter, for the ramekins

4 ripe-but-firm medium plums (about 1 pound total), pitted and cut into ½-inch chunks

About 1 tablespoon granulated sugar (depending on the sweetness of the plums)

½ teaspoon finely grated lemon zest

Kosher salt

One 8- to 10-ounce sheet frozen puff pastry, thawed

All-purpose flour, for rolling

½ cup almond frangipane (page 33)

2 tablespoons packed light or dark brown sugar

3 tablespoons sliced almonds

serves **8**

Position a rack in the center of the oven and heat the oven to 425°. Butter the inside of eight 6-ounce ramekins or custard cups; you can also use a muffin tin with large cups.

In a bowl, toss the plums with the sugar, lemon zest and a pinch of salt. Set aside to macerate, but not for more than 15 minutes or the fruit may release too much juice.

Lightly flour a work surface and roll the sheet of pastry into an 8-by-16-inch rectangle. Poke the pastry all over with a fork (or a pastry docker, if you're that kind of person), then cut the rectangle into eight squares.

Tuck a square of pastry into each ramekin, with the corners pointing up, pleating and folding as needed (you don't need to make these look perfect). Drop about a tablespoon of the frangipane into the center of each pastry cup, then pile the plums on top. Sprinkle each tart with some of the brown sugar and sliced almonds.

Bake until the pastry is deep golden brown, about 15 minutes. Reduce the heat to 350° and continue baking until a knife tip inserted into the center of the frangipane comes out clean, 10 to 15 minutes more. If the filling still seems runny but the pastry is browning too much, lower the heat even more. Let the tarts cool briefly in their molds, then pop them out and let them cool on a rack. They are best served just slightly warm or at room temperature on the day they're baked.

Almond Frangipane

This recipe produces more than you'll need for the plum tarts, but it's difficult to make a smaller batch in a food processor. Fortunately, frangipane freezes nicely, so scoop the remainder into a freezer bag and keep it at the ready for more desserts. It will stay good for up to two months.

½ cup slivered almonds

½ cup plus 2 tablespoons confectioners' sugar

¼ cup (½ stick) unsalted butter, at room temperature

1 tablespoon all-purpose flour

Kosher salt

¼ teaspoon pure vanilla extract

⅛ teaspoon almond extract

1 large egg

makes 1 cup

In a food processor, pulse the almonds until they're finely ground. Add the sugar, butter, flour, ¼ teaspoon of salt, the vanilla and almond extracts and pulse several more times to blend well. Add the egg and process until creamy. Scrape the frangipane into a bowl, cover and refrigerate until thickened and firm, at least 30 minutes.

Plum Galette with Gingersnaps

This rustic tart is my go-to dessert. Dinner with friends? Martha brings a galette! I make galettes with many fruits, but plums are ideal partners—I especially love the way heat transforms a plum. Colors grow vivid, juices get sticky and the flesh softens but doesn't get mushy the way a peach can. Galettes are great for those cooks who, like me, aren't particularly meticulous. There's no fluting or fussing required: just rolling an approximation of a round, piling on the plums and folding up the edge. The ginger-snap cookies (you can also use amaretti) soak up excess juices while also adding a hint of toasty ginger flavor.

2 cups plus 1 tablespoon unbleached all-purpose flour, divided, plus more for rolling

½ cup whole-wheat or rye flour

2 tablespoons plus ¼ cup sugar, divided

Kosher salt

1 cup plus 2 tablespoons cold unsalted butter, cut into small pieces

⅓ cup ice water

1½ pounds firm-ripe medium plums (about 6), pitted and cut into ½-inch slices

⅓ cup coarsely crushed ginger-snap cookies or amaretti

serves 6 to 8

In the bowl of a food processor, combine 2 cups of the all-purpose flour, the whole-wheat flour, 2 tablespoons of the sugar and ½ teaspoon of salt; pulse to blend. Add the butter and pulse until the largest piece of butter is the size of a small pea. With the processor running, drizzle in some of the ice water (don't add all the water yet). As you add the water, watch the dough: When the flour mixture starts to climb up the sides of the processor bowl, stop. Open the processor and carefully squeeze a big pinch of the dough between your fingers. If it holds together and feels moist, you don't need to mix any more. If it feels dry and powdery, pulse in a few more drops of water.

When the dough is the right consistency, transfer it to a floured work surface and knead it lightly by pushing the dough away from you with the heel of your hand and then gathering it back together. After a few strokes, shape it into a flat disk. Wrap the dough in plastic and chill for about 30 minutes; if you chill it for longer, let it warm up at room temperature for a few minutes before rolling.

Position a rack in the center of the oven and heat the oven to 375°.

In a medium bowl, toss the plums with the remaining 1 tablespoon of all-purpose flour and ¼ cup of sugar until combined.

Lightly flour your work surface again. Roll out the dough, turning and frequently sliding it on the work surface to prevent sticking, into a 15-inch circle about ⅛-inch thick. Gently roll the circle of dough around the rolling pin, position the pin over a large rimmed baking sheet lined with parchment or a nonstick baking mat, then unroll the dough onto the sheet. Center the dough in the baking sheet; it's okay if it hangs over the edge.

Sprinkle the gingersnap crumbs over the dough, leaving a 2-inch border. Pile the plum mixture in the center on top of the crumbs and fold the 2-inch border of the dough toward the center, loosely pleating as you go and pressing to repair any tears. Dot the exposed plums with the remaining 2 tablespoons of butter.

Bake the galette until the fruit is juicy and the crust is a deep golden brown on top and underneath (lift up an edge to check), 1 to 1¼ hours. Place the sheet with the galette on a rack and let it cool for at least 20 minutes before serving.

Plum & Pecan Puff Pastry Bands

I've made these flat tarts with Italian prune, Black Friars and Santa Rosas plums, and they were all delicious. The key is choosing a plum that's not too juicy. The tart looks stunning if you alternate the direction of the plums so that one row faces left and the next faces right. The thinner your slices, the neater the tarts will look, so take your time cutting the plums.

---

1 cup pecan halves or pieces

¼ cup unsalted butter, softened

¼ cup pure maple syrup (preferably grade B)

¼ cup sugar

1 tablespoon all-purpose flour, plus more for rolling

½ teaspoon ground cinnamon

½ teaspoon pure vanilla extract

Kosher salt

1 large egg

One 8- to 10-ounce sheet frozen puff pastry, thawed

2 ripe but not-too-juicy large plums (about 10 ounces), pitted and thinly sliced

makes 2 tarts

Position racks in the upper and lower thirds of the oven and heat the oven to 400°.

In a food processor, pulse the pecans until they're finely chopped but not powdery. Add the butter and pulse to blend. Add the maple syrup, sugar, flour, cinnamon, vanilla and a large pinch of salt and give it another pulse or two; add the egg and pulse until just blended.

Lightly flour a work surface and roll the puff pastry into a rectangle that's about 15 by 12 inches. Cut the dough in half to make two 15-by-6-inch rectangles.

Slide the pastry rectangles onto a large baking sheet lined with parchment or a nonstick baking mat (if you can fit both onto one sheet, great, but then reposition one oven rack in the center of the oven). Prick the pastry all over with a fork.

Spread half of the pecan mixture over one of the pastry rectangles, leaving a ½-inch border along each long side but spreading the mixture all the way to the edge of the short sides. Arrange the plums in neat rows with the fruit slightly overlapping, covering most of the filling but leaving a few gaps for the filling to show. Fold up the long sides over the edges of the plums to make a ½-inch border, pressing lightly with your fingers to flatten it a bit and make it stick to the plums. Prick the borders with the fork. Repeat with the second piece of dough, pecan mixture and plums.

Bake the tarts until the pastry is deep golden brown on the edges and the underside (lift it up to take a look) and the filling looks dry and shiny, 30 to 40 minutes. Slide the tarts onto a cooling rack and let cool until warm or room temperature. To serve, slice the tarts crosswise.

Prune & Armagnac Clafoutis

Here are three things I learned to love when I lived and studied cooking in France: prunes, good Armagnac and the super-simple batter pudding called clafoutis. The batter is like a crepe mixture—long on eggs, short on flour—and it's not very sweet. The sweetness comes from whatever fruit you choose. Cherry clafoutis is common in France, but I love substituting plums, either fresh or dried. In this version, the dried plums (aka prunes) are plumped up with Gascon Armagnac (or whatever brandy you have on hand), which gives the dessert a slightly grown-up character.

---

1 cup pitted prunes, halved

¼ cup Armagnac, Cognac or other brandy

4 tablespoons unsalted butter, divided, plus more for the pie plate

3 eggs

⅓ cup granulated sugar

1 teaspoon pure vanilla extract

¼ cup all-purpose flour

¾ cup half-and-half

2 tablespoons turbinado sugar (also called raw sugar, though it's not really)

serves
6

Soak the prunes in the Armagnac until they're soft and plump and have absorbed much of the liquor, about 1 hour. (It's okay if a bit of liquid is unabsorbed.) You can speed this step up by simmering the mixture very gently for a few minutes, to get the process started.

Heat the oven to 375°. Generously butter a 9-inch deep-dish pie plate. Melt 2 tablespoons of the measured butter and set aside.

Whisk the eggs, granulated sugar and vanilla together in a large bowl until they are frothy and the sugar has dissolved, about a minute with a hand whisk. Sprinkle in the flour and whisk until the mixture is smooth (you may have a few small lumps, but they'll disappear soon enough). Whisk in the half-and-half, a bit at a time, until you have a smooth batter. Finish by whisking in the melted butter.

Arrange the prunes in the prepared cake pan and drizzle any unabsorbed Armagnac over them. Pour the batter over the fruit and dot it with small bits of the remaining butter. Bake until puffed and golden brown and a skewer comes out clean, about 40 minutes. Immediately sprinkle with the turbinado sugar. Serve warm with a small glass of Armagnac on the side.

Plum & Prune Chutney

Using both fresh and dried plums (prunes) gives this chutney a full range of flavor, from bright to sticky-toffee sweet. Make sure you taste the finished chutney and adjust the ingredients to create a lively dance of vibrant flavors. I love this on cold roast pork or a ham sandwich with hot Dijon mustard. It's also nice on lighter food—as a topping for a grain and roasted vegetable salad, for example, or as a condiment for the best leftover in the world: a cold roasted chicken thigh.

1 tablespoon olive or vegetable oil

1 medium shallot, finely chopped

1 small fresh hot chile, seeded and minced

Kosher salt and freshly ground black pepper

½ cup dark brown sugar

½ cup sherry vinegar

2 tablespoons peeled minced ginger

1 whole clove

Half a stick of cinnamon

2 teaspoons brown mustard seeds

1½ pounds plums (about 6 medium), pitted and cut into ½-inch chunks

6 ounces pitted prunes, halved

makes 2 pints

Heat the oil in a large heavy-duty saucepan. Add the shallot and chile, season generously with salt and pepper and cook over medium heat until the shallot and chile have softened but not browned, about 2 to 3 minutes.

Add the sugar, vinegar, ginger, clove, cinnamon and mustard seeds. Stir and bring to a simmer. Add the plums, adjust the heat so the mixture still simmers and cook until the plums have broken down and the mixture thickens, about 15 minutes. Taste the chutney: If the cinnamon flavor is quite pronounced, remove the cinnamon stick. Add the prunes and continue cooking until they are soft and the whole mixture has a nice, thick texture. It should be like a chunky, loose jam; as it cools, the chutney will set up more.

Taste and adjust the spices so that the flavor is nicely balanced between heat, sweet, salty and fragrant spices. Cool and store in an airtight container in the refrigerator for up to 1 month.

Rosemary-Plum Shrub

Shrubs (also called drinking vinegars) are wonderful bases for homemade sodas or summer cocktails. But the true purpose of a shrub is to give the compulsive jam maker something else to do with seasonal fruit and sugar! It's a simple and quite lovely way to preserve the flavor of plums at their peak. In addition, if you add a ribbon and tag to a bottle of shrub, you've got a pretty gift to bring to a dinner party. White wine vinegar is a good neutral choice, but apple cider vinegar is nice as well. Sherry vinegar is delicious, but yields a deeper color and flavor.

---

1 pound very ripe red or purple plums (about 4 medium), pitted and cut into chunks

1 pound sugar (a bit more than 2 cups)

2 cups vinegar

One 5-inch sprig rosemary, rinsed and patted dry

In a large bowl, toss the plums with the sugar. Cover the bowl with a clean cloth and let sit at room temperature overnight. Give the mixture a stir once in a while to encourage the plums to release their juice. (If you find you've got a batch of plums that are reluctant to get juicy, transfer the mixture to a saucepan and heat gently until the fruit gets sloppier.)

Line a colander or a large strainer with cheesecloth and set it over a wide-mouth jar or a clean bowl. Ladle the plums and juice into the colander, letting the juice strain into the jar below. Press on the fruit to extract as much juice as possible, then discard the solids.

Add the vinegar to the juice, stir and taste the shrub: It should be quite tart, but should invite you to take another few sips. Stir in more sugar or vinegar to get the balance of sweet and tart you want.

Pour the shrub into a sterile bottle or jar, add the rosemary (cut it into pieces if you're using more than one jar) and seal. It will keep in the refrigerator indefinitely.

Plum-Raspberry Jam with Ginger & Cardamom

I always cross my fingers when I make jam: It's not easy to know whether the fruit has cooked enough to develop the body it needs to behave like a spreadable jam rather than a pourable sauce. But to be honest, it sort of doesn't matter: Whether your jam stands proudly on the spoon or drips over the edge, you'll find plenty of delicious destinations for it. For the most stunning color, use a deep red or purple plum.

---

2 pounds ripe medium plums, pitted and chopped (4 cups)

4 cups raspberries

4 cups sugar

2 tablespoons fresh lemon juice

½ teaspoon ground cardamom

2 tablespoons finely chopped peeled fresh ginger

2 tablespoons fresh lime juice

makes 5 half-pints

Boil 5 half-pint jars and their lids to sterilize them. Keep them in the hot water until you're ready to fill them with the jam.

Place the plums, raspberries, sugar and lemon juice in a large bowl. Let everything sit for a few hours at room temperature, tossing every so often to evenly distribute the sugar and macerate the fruit.

Pour the fruit mixture into a fine-mesh sieve over a large skillet and let the juice drain into the skillet. Set the fruit aside; it may have turned to mush, but that's okay. Bring the juice to a boil over medium-high heat. Reduce the heat and simmer for a few minutes until the juice has reduced by about half. Add the fruit, cardamom and ginger and return to a boil. Reduce the heat to maintain a simmer and cook until the mixture looks thick and a small amount dropped on a chilled saucer holds its shape when you draw your finger through it (or whatever other jam-testing method you use). Stir in the lime juice; taste and add a bit more if the jam is too sweet.

Remove the jars from the water and drain them. Divide the hot jam among the jars, leaving ¼ inch of room at the top. Wipe the rims clean, arrange the flat lids on top and lightly screw on the bands. Flip the jars upside down onto a dish towel. Let them sit for about 30 minutes, then turn them right side up. The lids should seal, making a satisfying popping sound, within a few hours. If they don't, either refrigerate the jam and use it within a few weeks or process the jars using the boiling-water method to reseal them (check a canning book for the precise method).

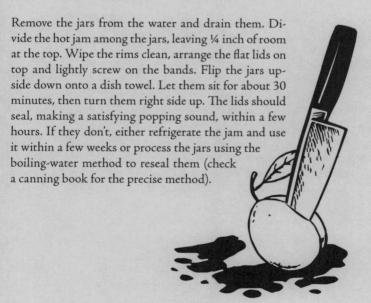

Thank You!

Thanks—as always—to my talented teammates Denise Mickelsen, for bringing her sharp eye to my text, and TaMara Edens, for testing many of these recipes. And thanks to my husband, Craig Umanoff, for planting those lovely plum trees.

—Martha Holmberg

Share your Short Stack cooking experiences with us
(or just keep in touch) via:

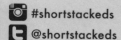 #shortstackeds   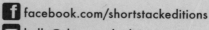 facebook.com/shortstackeditions
@shortstackeds   hello@shortstackeditions.com

Colophon

This edition of Short Stack was printed by Circle Press in New York City on Neenah Astrobrights Rocket Red (interior) and Neenah Oxford White (cover) paper. The main text of the book is set in Futura and Jensen Pro, and the headlines are set in Lobster.

Sewn by: *B I D*

Available now at ShortStackEditions.com: